Festivals

CHRISTMAS

Alan Blackwood

Wayland

Festivals

Buddhist Festivals
Christmas
Easter
Hallowe'en
Harvest and Thanksgiving

Hindu Festivals
Jewish Festivals
Muslim Festivals
New Year
Sikh Festivals

First published in 1984 by
Wayland (Publishers) Limited
49 Lansdowne Place, Hove
East Sussex BN3 1HF, England

Second impression 1985

ISBN 0 85078 450 6

Phototypeset by The Grange Press, Southwick, Sussex
Printed in Italy by G. Canale & C.S.p.A., Turin
Bound in the U.K. at The Pitman Press, Bath

Contents

The Christmas spirit

Christmas is the best-known, best-loved time of the year, all over the world. In London, Paris, New York, Tokyo, Sydney, in cold countries and hot ones, the people all wish each other a 'Merry Christmas!'

Christmas is a very important part of the Christian religion. Other religions have important festivals, too, but none that mean so much to so many people as Christmas.

There are good reasons for this. Christianity grew up mainly among the peoples and nations of Europe. When Europeans – the British, French, Spanish, Portuguese and Dutch – started to explore other parts of the world and to create empires, they took the Christian religion with them. That is how Christianity spread worldwide.

The reason why it has become the most popular time of year for everybody is easy to understand. It is a time of giving and receiving gifts, meeting friends, remembering others, eating well and having fun. Everybody, of whatever race or colour, likes the idea of peace and good will; Father Christmas; sparkling lights in shops and

Father Christmas is a popular figure the world over.

4

on Christmas trees; Christmas carols and pretty greetings cards; and all the other jollity that makes up the Christmas spirit.

Christmas lights in New York, U.S.A.

So, that is Christmas as we all know it today. But was it always like this? How did it begin?

The story of Christmas

Christ's birthday

The word 'Christmas' comes from 'Christ's Mass' – the special church service which celebrates the birth of Jesus Christ, the founder of Christianity. This is what the festival of Christmas is about.

The four Gospels in the New Testament of the Bible tell the story of Christ's birth. His parents, Joseph and Mary, were Jews, living in a land named Judaea, in the same region of the Middle East as the modern state of Israel. Judaea was a part of the Roman Empire, and Joseph and Mary had travelled to the small town of Bethlehem to register their names with the Roman authorities. Because the town was crowded, they had to stay in a stable. That is where Jesus Christ was born, among the cattle and other farmyard animals.

According to the Bible, his birth was a miracle, because Mary was still a virgin. The Bible also says that this miracle was known by three 'wise men', or astrologers, who followed a bright star that led them to the stable. There, they presented gifts to the new-born child. It also describes how an angel appeared in a vision to shepherds in the hills around Bethlehem, and told them that a marvellous Messiah, or holy leader, had been born.

All these happenings are remembered in

Mary, Joseph and the baby Jesus.

thousands of beautiful paintings, pieces of stained glass, and other works of art.

The date of Christmas Day is now 25 December. But nobody knows for certain if that is really Christ's birthday. Why, then have we chosen it?

The Nativity is often remembered in beautiful stained-glass windows like this one.

The Roman Saturnalia

December in the northern half of the world – the northern hemisphere – is the month of the winter solstice. This is the time of the year when the sun is at its closest to the horizon, before starting to climb higher again, each day, in the sky. In times past, when the light and warmth of the sun was a matter of life and death for many people, this passing of the winter solstice was a cause of much rejoicing.

The Roman people themselves called it *Dies Natalis Invicti Solis* – the Birthday of the Unconquered Sun. They marked the event with a festival called the Saturnalia. This was named after Saturn, their god of agriculture – since the gradual return of sunny days meant the beginning of a new farming year.

A merry time was had by all at the Roman Saturnalia.

The Roman Saturnalia was a big public holiday, marked by special events. People gave each other presents, children were often given pretty little wax dolls, and there were feasts. During the time of the Saturnalia, no war was declared, no battles fought, and nobody was sent to prison or otherwise punished. Slaves ate and drank with their masters. It was a time of happiness and good will.

The Christian religion grew up within the Roman Empire. To the early leaders of the Christian Church, it seemed a good idea to celebrate Christ's birthday on the occasion of such a popular and happy festival. That is one reason why we still celebrate Christmas in the middle of the winter, on the day that is now 25 December.

The Temple of Saturn in Rome, Italy.

The yule log

There were other ancient customs connected with this time of the winter solstice that also became a part of Christmas. In northern parts of Europe, where the winters were colder and darker than those in Roman Italy, people burnt giant logs of wood. These not only kept them warm, but were meant to beckon the sun to start rising in the sky once more.

The burning of the yule log – nobody is sure how it got this name – was quite a ceremony. The log was often decorated with ribbons, and people lined up to drag it home. When the log was burning, portions of its ash were scooped up and mixed with corn seed as a good luck charm. The final charred remains of the great yule log were placed in a jar or box, to protect the home from evil, and then used to help kindle the next winter's log.

The yule log was an important part of the Christmas festivities.

10

People in times long past were also struck by the fact that a few trees and shrubs did not loose their leaves in winter. To them, this was a wonderful sign that life was continuing, though the days were short and the nights long and cold. So they decorated their homes with sprigs of such evergreens as holly and ivy. Mistletoe, a plant which lives on other trees and bushes, was also regarded as a good luck charm in the home.

Even when Christianity became widespread, the people did not give up such ancient customs and beliefs. Besides, yule log fires and greenery in the home brought comfort and cheer at Christmas time.

Druids gathering mistletoe for the festival of the winter solstice.

Eating and drinking

Traditional brews

Since the days of the Roman Saturnalia, the Christmas season has always been a time for eating and drinking – a good way for people in the northern part of the world to keep up their strength and spirits during the gloomiest time of the year.

A great favourite with everybody in days gone by was the wassail bowl. The word 'wassail' comes from the old Saxon phrase, *wes hal*, meaning 'be whole', or 'good health!'

The wassail bowl was often as large as a

An old print of Father Christmas holding the wassail bowl.

cauldron. It was filled with such ingredients as cider, brandy, ale and spices, and often hung by a chain above the burning yule log till its contents bubbled merrily.

In courts and castles, the local lord usually provided the wassail 'brew', and invited all his friends, neighbours and servants to join him in drinking each other's health. Sometimes, people took the wassail bowl, decorated with ribbons, from house to house round the village, inviting everyone to have a drink, and then top up the bowl with drink of their own.

One of the best-known traditional brews of the wassail bowl was a kind of punch called lambs-wool. This included ale, roasted apples, sugar or honey, eggs, cream and portions of toasted bread.

An even more ambitious recipe included port, sherry, sugar, cloves, nutmeg, ginger, cinnamon, coriander and whipped eggs, all 'boiled up to a fine froth'. Then it was time to toss in soft, roasted apples, and serve!

A group of costumed performers – mummers – entertaining interested onlookers.

13

This 1907 print shows villagers buying their Christmas turkey or goose at a market.

The main dish

Roast swans, geese, capons (specially fattened chickens), pheasants and peacocks were at one time all important items on the Christmas menu. The way to prepare a pheasant was to remove the plumage as carefully as possible, put it aside while the bird was being cooked, then replace it before setting down the dish upon the Christmas table. It must have made a splendid sight.

The most celebrated dish, though, used to be roast boar's head. This was served with great ceremony. The head was decorated with holly, and an apple, orange or lemon stuck in its mouth. This tradition is carried on at Queen's College,

Oxford. The head is brought to the table on a very old silver dish, given to the college in 1668. Trumpeters announce its arrival, and a choir sings its praises.

Today, it is roast turkey that most of us sit down to on Christmas Day. The turkey's original home was North America. It was discovered by early European explorers, soon after the time of Columbus and the Pilgrim Fathers. A few turkeys were sent back to Europe, to Spain and to England, and by about 1650, turkeys had already become a popular Christmas dish. The English King, George II, kept about 3,000 turkeys in Richmond Park, near London, to feed his friends and guests at Christmas time.

Mince pies originally contained minced or chopped pieces of meat. They were often oblong in shape, to remind everyone of the crib in the stable at Bethlehem, and sometimes also had a little pastry image of the infant Jesus on top.

The boar's head was the most celebrated of Christmas dishes.

15

Other Christmas fare

Up to about a hundred years ago, one of the best-known Christmas foods was a dish called frumenty – a cross between a soup and a sauce. It was made from grains of wheat, boiled up into a broth, to which were added crushed almonds, milk and egg yolks. Many people ate frumenty, sweetened with honey or sugar, first thing on Christmas morning, and again just before going to bed. It was also served up with venison (deer meat), or mutton.

Another popular old Christmas food was plum porridge or plum pottage. This was a thick soup made by boiling up portions of beef or mutton with raisins, currants, and bread crumbs, and

A Victorian cartoon showing the after-effects of eating too much Christmas pudding!

So they agree to stay and dine at the host's table. An excellent dinner is served, and the grim faces of the old curmudgeons somewhat relax at sights of the turkey and the chine; while the arrival of the plum-pudding and a glance from the eldest Miss Posey cause to

seasoned with spices and wine. The so-called 'plum' part of it was provided by dried plums or prunes.

What we now know as Christmas pudding is more recent in origin. Some people still call it 'plum pudding', though nowadays it has no proper plums at all. Traditionally, it was steam-cooked in a cloth, giving it the shape and size of a football.

The rich, dark-brown Christmas pudding is a favourite with British people. Other countries have their own specialities in the way of puddings, cakes and sweets. In West Germany and France, they love marzipan – a sort of thick almond and sugar paste. Gingerbread was also an old-time favourite, often covered with icing sugar, and baked in the shape of St. Nicholas, or some other well-loved character.

The Christmas dinner has always been a favourite part of Christmas.

Fun and joy

Carol singing

Early on in the history of Christianity, there were special Christmas hymns. But these were only chanted in church, and had Latin words, which most people did not understand.

What were then called carols, were a popular type of song that people danced to as they sang. By about the year 1300, they started putting words in everyday language to some of the carol tunes, describing the Christmas story.

Carol singing adds to the spirit of fun and joy at Christmas.

Priests and scholars in the Church did not always approve of this idea of singing religious words to popular tunes. They said that some of the old carol tunes and dances went back to pagan times, and that it was sinful to put Christian words to them. On the other hand, carols were a good way of making the Christian teachings about Christ's birth more popular to the majority of people.

One or two of these old carols have come down to us, such as, *The Holly and the Ivy* which, in fact, has pagan words as well as a pagan tune. But nearly all today's best-known carols, such as, *O Come All Ye Faithful*, *Hark the Herald Angels Sing* and *O Little Town of Bethlehem*, have been composed much more recently.

The words of the beautiful carol, *Silent Night*, were written by an Austrian priest, Father Joseph Mohr, in 1818. The melody was added by the local organist, Franz Gruber. And because the local church organ had broken down at the time, he originally composed his melody for the guitar.

At Christmas, churches are often gaily decorated with trees and lights.

19

Good King Wenceslas

A very popular carol is *Good King Wenceslas*. This has an interesting history. An English clergyman, the Revd. John Neale, who lived a little over a hundred years ago, discovered a very old collection of songs. One of these had a march-like tune, probably intended for dancing. The Revd. Neale then wrote new words to this tune, so giving us *Good King Wenceslas*.

The words tell of King Wenceslas setting out in the snow with his page, to give food and shelter to a poor man on the Feast of Stephen – the earliest Christian saint, whose feast day is 26 December. The real Wenceslas, who lived over a thousand years ago, was not really a king. He was a prince of Bohemia – now a part of Czechoslovakia – who converted his country to Christianity. He was murdered by his evil brother, and buried in St. Vitus's Cathedral, Prague, which then became a famous place for pilgrims to visit.

Carol singers love *Good King Wenceslas* because of its good, sturdy tune. Years ago, long before there was radio, television, records or cassettes, carol singers provided a lot of the music at Christmas time. They went round towns and villages, often accompanied by musicians. These groups of carol singers and musicians were called waits. Nobody is sure of the meaning of 'wait'. It may have been a nickname for some of the wind instruments the musicians played, such as the crumhorn and the serpent.

A 1932 magazine cover showing Good King Wenceslas and his page trudging through the snow.

Right *An old print showing rival waits fighting in the snow.*

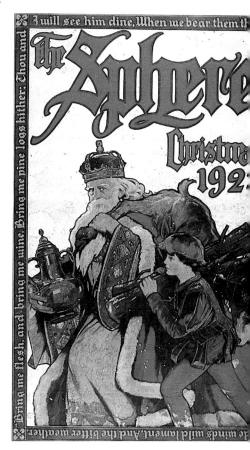

Scenes of the Nativity

Another Christmas feature, going back to the time of the Middle Ages, is the crib, or *crèche* (a French word meaning 'cradle') – a re-creation of the scene in the stable.

The idea belongs to St. Francis of Assisi. When he lived – from about 1182 to 1226 – few people could read or write. Church paintings and stained glass showed them the Bible stories in pictures. St. Francis decided to add to this method of instruction. He created a setting for the stable at Bethlehem, like a scene from a play. The infant Jesus lying in his wooden crib was a wax model. But the parts of Mary and Joseph, and the shepherds, were represented by real people. Live

A seventeenth-century tapestry of St. Francis of Assisi.

A Christmas crib re-creating the Nativity scene.

animals, including an ox and an ass, were also included in his Nativity scene.

It made such a deep impression on all who saw it, that St. Francis's idea quickly spread. At first, it was churches in Italy itself and in other Roman Catholic countries that displayed model cribs at Christmas time. Today, they are popular all over the world, in churches, shop windows, and people's own homes. Most cribs also have the Three Wise Men, dressed in all their fine clothes. In France, they often add figures of local craftsmen and tradesmen, such as a baker and a carpenter.

Some of the most attractive cribs are to be seen in the United States. The town of Bethlehem, Pennsylvania, lives up to its name with a beautiful crib in one of its churches. In other American towns and cities, there are open-air Nativity scenes, called Christmas Gardens.

Christmas trees

Queen Victoria, Prince Albert and their children round a Christmas tree.

For most of us, a fir tree sparkling with lights is the prettiest part of Christmas.

The story of Christmas trees started in Germany, a land famous for its deep, dark forests. The reason for choosing fir trees goes back over a thousand years, to the time when the Christian missionary, St. Boniface, was preaching in pagan Germany. One day, he cut down an oak tree that had been used for pagan worship. According to legend, he was amazed to see a young fir tree spring up from its roots. This he took to be a marvellous sign of the Christian faith.

The great German religious leader, Martin Luther, may have created the first true Christmas tree. The story about him says that he took a fir tree home, and lit it with candles to remind him of the starry sky over Bethlehem on the night Christ was born.

German soldiers, fighting with the British in the American War of Independence in 1776, introduced Christmas trees to America. The German-born Prince Albert, who married Queen Victoria in 1840, certainly helped to make them popular in Britain.

Not all Christmas trees are in people's homes. One famous one, in America, grows outside the White House, in Washington DC, and its lights are switched on each Christmas time by the President. Another giant one stands in London's Trafalgar Square, sent each year by the people of Oslo, the capital of Norway.

A giant Christmas tree standing in New York, U.S.A.

Christmas cards and crackers

People have been giving each other gifts at Christmas time ever since the days of the Roman Saturnalia. But the custom of sending Christmas greetings cards only began about a hundred and fifty years ago.

When Sir Rowland Hill reformed Britain's postal services in 1840, it became much easier and cheaper to send letters and cards by post. One of those who helped to administer the new post was a civil servant, Sir Henry Cole, and it was he who probably thought of the first Christmas card. This was decorated with vine leaves and showed people drinking a cup of good cheer. It was made in 1843.

Soon after, people everywhere were sending each other Christmas greetings cards. Some were most elaborate. They had little bunches of dried flowers attached, or they were designed to open

The first Christmas card was designed for Sir Henry Cole in 1843.

A Victorian picture of children pulling a cracker.

up and take the form of miniature churches or houses. Today, about 700 million Christmas cards are sold each year in Britain alone.

The original idea for Christmas crackers came from France, where little bags of sweets were wrapped in such a way that they had to be tugged hard before they broke open. A London pastry cook, Thomas Smith, saw some of these, then had the idea for a true cracker, after he had sat watching the logs crackle and snap in his fireplace. He also thought of putting small toys and mottoes inside his crackers. That was in 1860.

One of the largest Christmas crackers was made for a Victorian pantomime. It was over two metres long, and contained new costumes for the cast, as well as dozens of smaller crackers to be thrown to the audience. It must have made quite a bang!

Who was Father Christmas?

Santa Claus

Nowadays, we think of Santa Claus and Father Christmas as being the same person. Going back in history and legend, we find that they were quite different characters.

The name 'Santa Claus' is the old Dutch word for 'St. Nicholas', a man who lived in Turkey, about 1500 years ago. He was one of the first bishops of the Christian Church, and was imprisoned for a while by the Romans because of his faith.

St. Nicholas is the patron saint of Russia (as St. George is for England). But he is best remembered for his kindness towards children. One story says that he gave some gold to a poor father, to save his three young daughters from poverty and shame. Another quite grim story says he discovered the remains of three young lads, who had been murdered and cut up into pieces by a wicked innkeeper. St. Nicholas is supposed to have put the pieces together again, and brought the boys back to life.

Owing to these legends, St. Nicholas also became the patron saint of children. His feast day was close to Christmas time, and the tradition grew up that he gave presents to children.

In some countries, the children were told that

St. Nicholas, the patron saint of children and of Russia.

St. Nicholas had a companion who went ahead of him, and found out whether they had been good or bad during the year. The saint only visited the homes of those who had been good.

It was believed that he travelled about on a donkey, and sometimes people in France and other countries still leave a little bundle of hay by the fireplace as a treat for the animal!

An Australian Father Christmas listening to what this small child wants for his Christmas present.

Mythical figures

The character we know as Father Christmas is closely connected with the old pagan religions.

In the days before Christianity became widespread, the people of northern Europe believed in many gods and goddesses. One of these gods was called Odin. He was believed, at the time of the winter solstice, to ride across the sky on a magic horse, punishing the wicked and rewarding the good with gifts.

Odin, the northern god who rode across the sky on a magic horse.

A Swiss Father Christmas with a long beard and red coat.

Another very old, mythical figure connected with winter time, has been described in different forms. Sometimes he was described as a kind of dwarf in a red cloak with a hood – the colour red was probably inspired by the cheerful red berries on the holly trees. Sometimes he was said to be a tall figure, with a snow-white cloak and a long, white beard. A third version of this strange, but friendly, figure was dressed in a green robe, with a crown of holly or ivy on his head, and a yule log strapped to his back. In his hands he carried a bowl of some delicious sweet punch for everyone to drink. Whatever form he took, this character was supposed to have brought people warmth and cheer at the coldest, darkest time of year.

When Christianity came to Europe, people did not forget about Odin, or the other age-old characters. They added them to their idea of Christmas.

The Lord of Misrule

Yet another figure of the past connected with Christmas time, was called the Lord of Misrule.

In the courts of medieval kings, princes and barons, someone was chosen, at the start of the Christmas season, to be the Lord of Misrule – a kind of special court jester. One way of choosing him was to make a cake with a ring hidden inside it. Whoever got the slice of cake with the ring, was Lord of Misrule.

His duties were to organize the Christmas festivities. He thought up games and jokes and comic plays for everyone to act in. During the Christmas period, the Lord of Misrule ran the court. The king, or lord and lady of the manor, joined in the fun with their servants – just as the masters and slaves joined together in the celebrations at the time of the Roman Saturnalia.

The Lord of Misrule (left) was a kind of court jester.

The Lord of Misrule often took part in the traditional Christmas mummer's plays. In them St. George always had his famous battle with the dragon – a contest symbolizing the victory of the sun over the darkness of winter.

So it was, over the centuries, that the familiar figure of our own Father Christmas gradually took shape. St. Nicholas, or Santa Claus, brings presents for the children. Odin's magic horse has given us the idea of a sleigh, and team of reindeer flying across the sky. The other strange old figures of pagan times have added the red cloak, white hair and beard. The Lord of Misrule has brought jollity and fun to Father Christmas.

Mummers performing the battle between St. George and the dragon amid noisy merrymaking.

The Christmas season

Advent

Advent is the time of year leading up to the 'arrival' of Christ's birthday – that is, Christmas Day. A traditional Advent custom is the special kind of calendar, made in the shape of a little cardboard house. Behind each window is a verse from the Bible, or a picture. The windows are meant to be opened one by one, as Christmas Day draws near.

Christmas Eve, coming at the end of Advent, is a time of great excitement. In olden days, it was also thought to be a time of strange happenings.

The special Christmas Eve game of snapdragon.

Pantomimes – a kind of play performed at Christmas time – are popular in Britain.

People believed that cattle knelt down at midnight in honour of Christ's birth, or that they received the gift of speech. But woe betide anyone who saw or heard such wonders, for they would die within the year. There was another belief, that on Christmas Eve the burning yule log cast people's shadows on the wall. Those whose shadow had no head would also die soon!

Girls used to bake what were called dumb cakes on Christmas Eve. They had to prepare the cake and put it in the oven, all on their own and without uttering a sound. Then, so they hoped, their future husband would come in through the kitchen door.

There was a special Christmas Eve game as well, called snapdragon. Raisins were put in a bowl, and brandy poured over them. The brandy was set alight, and those gathered round had to try and pick out a raisin from the flickering blue flames. The game was played in the dark, to add to the magical atmosphere of Christmas Eve.

Boxing Day

Boxing Day – the day after Christmas – is quite different from Christmas Eve. It is also the old feast day of St. Stephen. St. Stephen is connected with the health and care of horses, though this is because he got mixed up with another St. Stephen, who was a Christian missionary in Sweden. Despite this mistake, it is the Feast of Stephen on 26 December that has long been a day for outdoor sports with horses, such as hunting and racing.

At one time, it was also the day for a sport known as hunting the wren. People tried to catch the little birds and put them in cages. This sport goes back to the druids of pagan times, who believed they could foretell the future by listening to the wren's song.

Hunting the wren was a popular sport in times past.

An old cartoon about Boxing Day. How many things can you see connected with the word 'box'?

Boxing Day may have taken its name from the fact that, at one time, alms boxes were placed in churches at Christmas. Alms were gifts for the poor, usually in the form of money. The boxes were opened the day after Christmas Day, and the money distributed among the poor people of each parish.

The name may also be connected with the old earthenware 'boxes' in which servants and trades people collected their Christmas gifts of money. They had to break these open to get the money out again, and the day for doing this was 'Boxing Day'. Some people still talk about giving 'Christmas boxes' to the postman, and others who provide a service through the year.

New Year's Eve

All over the world, at midnight on New Year's Eve, bells ring out to welcome in the New Year. At parties, people join hands and sing *Auld Lang Syne*. This old Scots song reminds us that in Scotland, especially, New Year celebrations are as important as those of Christmas itself. Four hundred years ago, the Puritans tried to put an end to Christmas merry-making in Scotland, so the people celebrated New Year instead.

The Scots call their New Year festivities, Hogmanay. This word may come from an old French expression about mistletoe, and dates from the time when France and Scotland were allies against England.

One old Hogmanay custom is to do with 'burning up' the last of the old year, before the

New Year's Eve has always been a time for enjoying yourself.

new one arrives. In the towns, people sometimes carry a blazing tar barrel through the streets. In some fishing villages, they set light to a boat, to symbolize the end of the old year.

Another Scottish New Year tradition, once taken very seriously, was called first-footing. After midnight had struck, those who stayed at home waited anxiously for the first stranger to knock on their door and enter. If it was a black headed man bearing a small gift, or a sprig of mistletoe, then all would be well for the coming year. If, on the other hand, the first stranger of the new year was a woman, or someone lame, flat-footed or blind in one eye, then, so it was feared, bad luck lay ahead.

The first-footing is still practised in some parts of Scotland.

39

The Feast of Epiphany

One more important day connected with Christmas, is the Feast of the Epiphany. This is a Greek word meaning 'manifestation', and it describes the presentation of the infant Jesus to the Three Wise Men. They, in their turn, presented to him gifts of gold, frankincense and myrrh. Nobody knows who these three 'wise men', 'kings', or 'magi' really were, or where they came from; but for hundreds of years they have been called Melchior, Caspar and Balthazar.

The Three Wise Men following the star that led them to the stable where Jesus was born.

The Feast of the Epiphany is 6 January. At one time, this was the date of Christmas Day itself. Now it is the twelfth and last day of the whole Christmas season. Twelfth Night used to be a time for special fun and games. Cakes were baked, containing a single bean. Whoever got the bean in their slice, became the Bean King – rather like the ring in the cake as a way of choosing the Lord of Misrule. Others then became members of the Bean King's 'court', and given such comical names as Sir Gregory Goose and the Duchess of Daffodil. Everybody dressed up in fancy clothes.

In some countries, Epiphany is still a big event. In Italy, they remember a kindly witch called Befana, who was supposed to have helped the Three Wise Men find their way to the stable. Children wait for her to bring them presents, just like Father Christmas.

Burning the Christmas decorations. It is supposed to be bad luck to have your house decorated after Twelfth Night.

Christmas round the world

In Mexico, children play a game called *pinãta* on Christmas Day. Large earthenware jars, decorated with tinsel, and filled with sweets, are suspended from the ceiling. Each child is then blindfolded, and tries to hit and break open one of the jars with a stick. The winner gets a special prize, and the sweets are shared out.

In the southern hemisphere, Christmas comes in midsummer, when the weather is hottest and trees and shrubs are all in bloom. In New Zealand, the people sometimes use a blossoming tree called the pohutukawa instead of the traditional Christmas fir tree. In Australia, they have a

Christmas festivities in Perth, Australia. Christmas comes during the summer months in the southern hemisphere.

lovely flower called the Christmas bell – a bell-shaped yellow bloom surrounded by bright green leaves.

Australians still eat roast turkey, Christmas pudding and mince pies. But many take their Christmas dinner to a sandy beach instead of having it at home.

In large parts of the world today, there is no official religion, and Christmas is not a special holiday. But many old Christmas customs are remembered. In the Ukraine, which is part of the Soviet Union, they still prepare a special feast of twelve courses – one course in honour of each of Christ's twelve disciples. As evening approaches, a child of each household looks out for the first star to appear in the sky. This is the signal for the feast to begin. And in the Soviet Union as a whole, Father Christmas – known as Grandfather Frost – still brings Christmas cheer and gifts to millions of children.

A street in Tokyo, Japan, during Christmas week.

Christmas in Bethlehem

One of the most holy places at Christmas time today is the town of Bethlehem, in Israel. Each year, people from all over the world visit the scene of the very first Christmas.

The climax to Christmas in Bethlehem is the service held in the Church of the Nativity, on Christmas Eve. A church was built on the site in about the year AD 330, during the reign of Constantine – the first Roman emperor to become a Christian. This was destroyed, but another church was built in about the year AD 550, in the time of the Emperor Justinian; and this is the one that still stands. It is the oldest Christian church still in use, anywhere in the world.

The grotto of the Nativity in Bethlehem, Israel.

Priests holding a service in the Church of the Nativity on Christmas Eve.

Beneath it is the cave or grotto of the Nativity. In this small shrine, a silver star set in the stone floor marks what is believed to be the actual spot where Christ was born. Above it are fifteen silver lamps that represent the various branches of the Christian faith.

On 24 December, hundreds of Roman Catholic and Protestant pilgrims visit the grotto, then crowd into the small church for the Christmas Eve service. Another ceremony takes place on 6 January, when the Eastern Orthodox Church still celebrates Christmas.

Thousands more people gather in the hills around Bethlehem on Christmas Eve, at the place they think the shepherds had their marvellous vision of the angel announcing to them Christ's birth, nearly two thousand years ago.

Glossary

Astrologers Those who try to foretell events by studying the position of the planets and stars in the sky.

Druids Priests of the old pagan religions of Western Europe.

Feast day A joyous religious festival. In the Roman Catholic Church, the memory of many saints was traditionally honoured with a public holiday, with feasting and dancing.

Gospels The first four books of the Bible's New Testament, namely Matthew, Mark, Luke and John.

Mummers A group of masked performers in a folk play or mime.

Nativity The word describing the event of Christ's birth.

Pagan A heathen; primitive religions not based on a belief in God.

Pilgrim Fathers The English Puritans – Protestants who led very simple and 'pure' lives – who sailed across the Atlantic in 1620, to create a new colony for themselves in North America.

Saturnalia An ancient Roman festival held at the same time of the year as Christmas, in honour of Saturn, their god of agriculture.

Winter solstice In the northern hemisphere, the day when the sun is at its lowest point above the horizon at noon.

Yule log A large log of wood traditionally used as the foundation of a fire in the hearth at Christmas.

Further reading

If you would like to find out more about Christmas, you may like to read the following books:

Christmas Customs and Folklore by Margaret Baker (Shire, 1972)

A Christmas Book by Diane Elson (World's Work Ltd., 1980)

An Old-fashioned Christmas by Iris Grender (Hutchinson, 1979)

The Oxford Christmas Book for Children by Roderick Hunt (O.U.P., 1981)

A Treasury of Christmas by Frank and Jamie Muir (Robson Books, 1981)

The Christmas Book by James Reeves (Heinemann, 1975)

The Long Christmas by Ruth Sawyer (Bodley Head, 1972)

Index

Acknowledgements

The publisher would like to thank all those who provided pictures on the following pages: BBC Hulton Picture Library 24; British Tourist Authority 39; D. Pike 44, N. O. Tomalin 5, 25 – Bruce Coleman Limited; Mary Evans Picture Library 6, 14, 15, 16, 17, 18, 20, 21, 22, 26, 27, 28, 32, 34, 37, 40, 41; Sonia Halliday Photographs 7; Alan Hutchison Library 29; The Mansell Collection 8, 10, 12, 30, 33, 38; Peter Newark's Western Americana 11; Outlook Films Ltd. 19, 31; Ann & Bury Peerless 23; Picturepoint Ltd. 9, 35, 42, 43, 45; TOPHAM 4; ZEFA cover.